Audubon's
BIRDS

The Natural History Museum Library

Audubon's
BIRDS

A selection of the magnificent illustrations by
JOHN JAMES AUDUBON
first published 1827-1838

MALLARD PRESS

Mallard Press and its accompanying design and logo
are trademarks of BDD Promotional Book Company, Inc.

Copyright © 1991 Wordsworth Editions Ltd.

First published in the United States of America
in 1992 by The Mallard Press.

ISBN 0-7924-5580-0

Printed and bound in Hong Kong by South China Printing Co.

Acknowledgements

The publishers would like to thank the many people at the Natural History Museum, London, who made publication of this book possible; in particular Rex Banks, Head of Library Services, Librarians Anne Datta and Carol Gokce, together with Tim Parmenter and his staff in the Photographic Department.

Introduction

JOHN JAMES AUDUBON 1785-1851, 'the American Woods-man', was the illegitimate son of Jean, a French naval officer-cum-planter, and Jeanne Rabine, a Creole from Santo Domingo (now Haiti). John's mother died soon after his birth, and when he was three he accompanied his father to France, to Nantes, where he was officially adopted by Jean and Jean's French wife Anne. In spite of the vicissitudes of the French Revolution, in which the Nantais suffered terribly, young John seems to have enjoyed the benefits of a bourgeois French provincial education, and at this time his love of nature first showed itself.

In 1803, John re-crossed the Atlantic to help manage his father's estate at Mill Grove, near Philadelphia. Here he met and married Lucy Bakewell, the daughter of an English neighbour. John and Lucy's early married life was spent running a store in Louisville, and in 1809 they were visited by a curious tinware pedlar who arrived with a parrot on his shoulder and a portfolio of ornithological drawings under his arm. This was the Scotsman Alexander Wilson, who was engaged in seeking subscribers for his *American Ornithology* (published in Philadelphia 1808-1814). Audubon readily subscribed in spite of his partner's objection that their money was required for useful articles, and that anyway, Audubon's own drawings were greatly superior to Wilson's. This is arguably true, and it seems to have been at the root of a smouldering animosity that Wilson felt towards Audubon; certainly Wilson's friends and patrons did little to help Audubon's own publishing plans more than a decade later.

However, Wilson's visit fired Audubon's ambition, and he determined to surpass him in ornithological achievement. Even the destruction by rats of many of his early drawings did not deter him, and he neglected family and business for a number of years so that he could spend time on his bird observations and drawings for his portfolio. It was during this period of backwoods wandering that he acquired his reputation as 'the American Woodsman', emulating the tradition of Crockett and Boone, both of whom he admired enormously. Financial necessity brought an end to his wanderings, and the early 1820s found him painting portraits and teaching art at the school in Louisiana that his wife Lucy had started.

By 1826, Audubon felt that he had enough drawings to embark on the quest for subscribers to his great work. He had decided that it was to be published in double elephant folio format (39½ x 27 inches) so that all the subjects could be reproduced life-size and in natural surroundings (even though this necessitated cunning convolutions of the necks of some of the larger birds). Neither subscribers nor sufficiently skilled engravers were to be found in the United States, and in May 1826 Audubon sailed for England.

The wild woodsman that landed in Liverpool must have presented a compelling sight in his buckskins and long, bear-greased locks. Perhaps this appearance was a form of salesmanship, because once he had established himself, Audubon reverted to the fashionable dress that he had affected in New Orleans. Anyway, he soon found a partner for his enterprise in William Home Lizars, an Edinburgh engraver. Lizars, however, produced only the first ten plates, because labour difficulties caused his withdrawal from the project. The remaining 425 plates were produced in London by the firm of Robert Havell, and the opus, *Birds of America*, was completed at last in June 1838. Between 175 and 200 copies were printed, and the text *Ornithological Biography* (1831-1839) appeared separately to avoid the compulsory deposit of the plates at the British Museum and other copyright libraries in Britain.

Following the successful publication of the double folio edition of *Birds of America* Audubon worked on an octavo edition with additional plates, completed in 1843 and published in Philadelphia, and *The Viviparous Quadrupeds of North America* (1842-1845) completed by Audubon's sons Victor and John Woodhouse Audubon. By now, Audubon had returned to the United States to make his home on the Hudson River, in the northern part of Manhattan Island.

Although Audubon's drawings and paintings may not wholly satisfy both the critical artist and the meticulous scientist, his achievements in both areas are considerable. Without doubt, they remain one of the great contributions to American natural history. The forty illustrations in this book owe much to modern methods of reproduction, which enable today's reader to appreciate the excellence of the original hand-coloured engravings. They are representative of the extraordinary range and quality of Audubon's masterwork, which embraced so many species and habitats.

The plates are reproduced from one of the two original sets of four elephant folios in the Natural History Museum, London.

Contents

An index by common name appears on the following leaf.

Alphabetical Index
by common name

Publisher's Note

The illustrations in this volume have been photographed directly from the pages of rare original editions held by the Natural History Museum Library. As these originals are filled with whole-page reproductions, and illustrations go into the gutters at the centre, this has inevitably resulted in slight curvature at the very edge of some colour plates, although this is only noticeable where captions and other text appear. Rather than remove this artificially by masking or other means, the publishers have decided to reproduce as much of the original page area as possible, both to do full justice to the paintings and for the historical and documentary information they contain.

Cooper's Hawk
Accipiter cooperi

COOPER'S HAWK has a wide range, breeding from British Columbia to Prince Edward Island and south to Mexico. Called the Stanley Hawk by Audubon, it winters from British Columbia and northern Maine to Mexico.

About seventeen inches long, it lives largely in woods, and because it is not commonly given to soaring, its arboreal habit often causes it to be overlooked. It feeds off a wide variety of prey, which includes small birds and mammals, reptiles, amphibians and large insects.

Stanley Hawk's Male 1. F. 2.
ASTUR STANLEII.

Whip-Poor-Will
Antrostomus vociferus

THE BREEDING RANGE of this bird is from North Dakota, Manitoba and Nova Scotia to Arizona and Georgia, and it winters further south from South Carolina and the Gulf states to Central America.

The Whip-Poor-Will is about ten inches long, and frequents thickets in woods, and as a result is much more likely to be heard than seen: its distinctive cry, which is a repeated utterance of its name, is unmistakeable. It feeds off insects, taken on the wing. The hen-bird usually lays two eggs on open ground or among dead leaves.

Whip-poor-will. Male 1. F. 2. 3.
quercus tinctoria.
Vulgo Black Oak.

Caprimulgus vociferus.

Drawn from Nature and Published by John J. Audubon F.R.S. F.L.S. &c.

Engraved, Printed & Coloured by R. Havell June. 1830.

Roseate Spoonbill

Ajaia ajaja

ROSEATE SPOONBILLS were formerly widespread, but because of the demand for their feathers, they were nearly exterminated in the first half of the twentieth century. Careful protection of the species has ensured its survival. The Roseate Spoonbill ranges from Texas, Louisiana and Florida south to Argentina and Chile.

It is about two-and-a-half feet long and inhabits swamps and marshes. It lays three to five eggs, usually in a heronry in the company of other birds. It feeds off fish, crustaceans, insects and water plants.

PLATE CCCXXI

Drawn from Nature by J. J. Audubon. F.R.S. F.L.S.

Engraved, Printed, and Coloured by R. Havell 1836

Roseate Spoonbill.
PLATALEA AJAJA. L.
Male. Adult.

Golden Eagle

Aquila chrysaetos

THIS RARE EAGLE breeds from Alaska and Mackenzie to Lower California and Oklahoma; formerly it used to extend its range to North Carolina. In winter, it may be found further south from Texas to Florida.

With a wing-spread of up to seven-and-a-half feet, the Golden Eagle inhabits remote mountains, where it lays two to three eggs in nests on cliffs. It is, perhaps, most likely to be seen in National Parks.

PLATE. CLXXXI.

Golden Eagle. AQUILA CHRYSAETOS. Female adult. Northern Hare.

Drawn from Nature by J.J.Audubon F.R.S. F.L.S.

Engraved, Printed & Coloured by R. Havell 1833.

Great Blue Heron

Ardea herodias

THIS LARGE HERON breeds from Alaska and Nova Scotia to Mexico and Bermuda, and winters from Alaska to southern New York state. Other races include Ward's Heron, Treganza's Heron, the Northwest Coast Heron and the California Heron.

In length, the bird is about four feet long with a wingspan of about six. It is slate-grey in colour, and is sometimes confused with cranes; however they may be easily distinguished in flight because herons fly with their neck folded whereas cranes fly with outstretched neck. The Great Blue Heron feeds principally off mice, fish and snakes.

PLATE. CCXI.

Drawn from Nature by J.J.Audubon. F.R.S. F.L.S.

Engraved, Printed & Coloured by R. Havell 1834.

Great blue Heron. ARDEA HERODIAS. *Male.*

Great White Heron

Ardea occidentalis

THIS STRIKING BIRD has immaculate white feathers with yellow-green bill and legs and is sometimes confused with the smaller American Egret, which, however, has black legs. It is confined almost exclusively to Florida Bay.

This is the largest American heron and measures about fifty inches, with a wing-spread of seven feet. It feeds off fish, crustaceans and molluscs, and lays three eggs on a platform in mangrove swamps. In former times it was nearly exterminated by sponge fishers who took its young for food.

PLATE CCLXXXI

Great White Heron. ARDEA OCCIDENTALIS. *Male adult spring plumage.* *Nat. Size.*

Goshawk

Astur atricapillus

THE NORTHERLY BREEDING EXTENT of the Goshawk is Alaska and the Labrador–Ungava peninsula, but it also breeds as far south as Maryland and Mexico. It winters throughout much of its range, to Mexico and Virginia, periodically moving south in considerable numbers.

It is about two feet in length, and has a typical hawk-like shape with short rounded wings and long tail. The adults are grey with a dark cap. In this plate, the bird on the right, called the Stanley Hawk by Audubon, is the same as Cooper's Hawk (see p. 14).

Goshawk.
FALCO PALUMBARIUS, Linn.
Adult Male 1. Young 2.

Stanley Hawk.
FALCO STANLEII, Aud.
Adult. 3.

Red-Shouldered Hawk
Bureo lineatus

RED-SHOULDERED HAWKS breed from Prince Edward Island and Ontario to Kansas, Tennessee, North Carolina and west to the edge of the Great Plains. They are also found in Texas, and there is a red-bellied variety in California. It winters from Iowa and New Hampshire to Mexico and the Gulf coast, and also in California.

It is about twenty inches in length, and is most likely to be seen soaring in open country near woodlands. Its principal prey is small rodents.

Red-shouldered Hawk.
Male 1. F. 2.
Falco lineatus.

Drawn from Nature and Published by John J. Audubon F.R.S.E. FL.S. M.W.S.   Engraved by R. Havell, Jun.ᵗ Printed & Coloured by R. Havell & S.ᵒⁿ London, 1829.

Swainson's Hawk

Buteo swainsoni

BRITISH COLUMBIA and Manitoba to Mexico is the principal breeding range of this hawk, which Audubon knew as the Common Buzzard. It winters in South America, generally south of the Equator.

Inhabiting prairies, plains and deserts, it preys off harmful rodents and reptiles, and may be thought to be beneficial to man, but it is frequently shot. A medium-sized hawk, it is about eighteen inches long. It lays two to four eggs in a bulky nest.

PLATE CCCLXXII

Drawn from Nature by J.J.Audubon, F.R.S. F.L.S.

Engraved, Printed and Coloured by R. Havell 1837.

Common Buzzard.
BUTEO VULGARIS.
Female
Marsh Hare. *Female.*
Lepus Palustris. Bachman.

Quail

Colinus cristatus, Oreortyx picta

IN NORTH AMERICA, the Quail is often known by the name of its genus, Partridge (*Perdix*), and that is the case with the illustration here. *Colinus cristatus* on the right of the plate is the Crested Colin, or Virginian Quail, which ranges from Guatamala southward to Venezuela and eastward to the Guianas and north-eastern Brazil. The other two birds are Mountain Quail, which range western North America from Washington through California to Mexico.

Unlike the Old World quail, American quail do not migrate, though they move from one feeding area to another in company with other birds in large coveys or flocks. They feed off harmful insects and some plant seeds. They may lay up to sixteen eggs.

PLATE CCCCXX

85.

Drawn from Nature by J. J. Audubon. F.R.S. P.L.S

Engraved Printed and Coloured by Rob.ᵗ Havell. 1838.

Plumed Partridge.
PERDIX PLUMIFERA, *Gould.*
2. Male. 3. Female.

Thick-legged Partridge.
PERDIX NEOXENUS, *Aud.*
1. Supposed Young Male.

Holboell's Grebe

Colymbus grisegna

Known by Audubon as the Red-necked Grebe, this wide-ranging bird breeds from Siberia and northern Canada to Washington and Minnesota. It winters mainly on coasts from Maine to North Carolina and British Columbia to California.

Although it will spend the winter offshore, in summer Holboell's Grebe inhabits marshes where it will build nests, frequently floating nests, in which it lays four to five eggs. It is about twenty-one inches long, and feeds off crustaceans, salamanders, insects and fish.

PLATE CCXCVII

Drawn from Nature by J. J. Audubon. F R S. F L S.

Engraved, Printed, & Coloured, by R. Havell 1836.

Red-necked Grebe.
PODICEPS RUBRICOLLIS, Lath.
1. Adult Male spring plumage. 2. Winter plumage.

Carolina Paroquet

Conuropsis carolinensis

THE CAROLINA PAROQUET or Parrakeet is now extinct, the last example having died in the Cincinnati Zoological Gardens in 1944. It was the only species of parrot found on the North American continent, and at one time large colonies often numbering several hundred were resident in forests from Nebraska and Ohio to Oklahoma and Florida.

About twelve inches long, the Parrakeets fed off seeds, fruit and berries, but were persecuted for depradation of cultivated crops, as well as being sought for capture as cage birds.

Carolina Parrot, Males 1 F. 2 Young 3

PSITACUS CAROLINENSIS,

Plant Vulgo, Cuckle Burr.

Drawn from Nature & Published by John J. Audubon. F.R.S.E. M.W.S.

Engraved, Printed, & Coloured by R. Havell & Son, London.

Raven

Corvus Corax

THIS GLOSSY BLACK scavenging bird ranges from Alaska and Greenland to Georgia and Nicaragua. There are also Eurasian races.

Living in remote forests and on sea coasts, especially where there are cliffs, ravens lay four to seven eggs in tree-tops or on rocky ledges. Their wingspan is frequently over four feet, and they have a gutteral croak. Ravens have been taught to mimic human speech, and have long been the subject of superstition and legend. They are omniverous.

Raven,
CORVUS CORAX,
Male.

Thick Shell-bark Hickory, Juglans laciniosa.

Drawn from nature by J.J. Audubon F.R.S. F.L.S.

Engraved, printed & Coloured by R. Havell, Jun.

Blue Jay
Cyanocitta cristata

THIS HANDSOME and familiar bird is a corvid and is therefore related to the crow, the raven and the magpie. It breeds from Nebraska, Alberta and Newfoundland to Texas and Florida. It ranges further south in winter.

The Blue Jay is about a foot in length, and inhabits woodland, parks and farms. As well as the blue and white coloration with the marked crest, it is distinguished by its harsh cry and imitative capability. In the breeding season however it has a bell-like song, almost as though two pieces of crockery were knocking together. It lays four to seven eggs in well-concealed nests, and feeds off insects, nuts, wild fruits, eggs and young birds.

Blue Jay,

CORVUS CRISTATUS,

Male. 1. Female. 2. 3.

Drawn from nature by J.J. Audubon F.R.S. F.L.S.

Engraved, printed & Coloured by R. Havell, Jun.

Black-throated Blue Warbler

Dendroica caerulescens

THE MALE WARBLER depicted here is easily distinguished from the hen bird, which is a nondescript brown. Ranging from Minnesota and Quebec to Georgia, the southern race is known as Cairns's Warbler.

Inhabiting woods, these five-inch long birds are largely insectivorous. They build open, cup-shaped nests at moderate heights but are favoured victims of the parasitic cowbird. Like other warblers, Black-throated Blue Warblers are unusual in that they can produce hybrids by mating with other species.

Black-throated Blue Warbler;
SYLVIA CANADENSIS. LATH.
Male
Canadian Columbine. Aquilegia canadensis.

Drawn from Nature by J.J.Audubon F.R.S. F.L.S.

Engraved, Printed & Coloured by R.Havell, London, 1832.

Warbler and Bluebirds

Dendroica townsendi, Sialia currucoides, Sialia mexicana

THE SMALL BIRD in this illustration (1) is Townsend's Warbler, which breeds from Prince William Sound and the upper Yukon to Washington, Alberta and Montana. It winters from California to Nicaragua.

The Mountain Bluebird (2 and 3), called here the Arctic Bluebird, breeds from Yukon and Manitoba to California and Chihuahua, and from Cascade Range and Sierra Nevada to North Dakota and Nebraska. It winters from California and Colorado to Lower California and Texas.

The Western Bluebird (4 and 5) breeds from British Columbia and Colorado to Mexico, and winters from California and Utah southwards.

PLATE CCCXCIII.

Drawn from Nature by J.J.Audubon F.R.S. F.L.S.

Engraved, Printed and Coloured by R.Havell. 1837.

Townsends Warbler.
SYLVIA TOWNSENDI, *Nuttall*
1. Male.

Arctic Blue-bird.
SIALIA ARCTICA, *Swain.*
2. Male. 3. Female.
Plant { Carolina Allspice.
CALYCANTHUS FLORIDÚS.

Western Blue-bird.
SIALIA OCCIDENTALIS, *Townsend.*
4. Male. 5. Female.

Passenger Pigeon

Ectopistes migratorius

THE PASSENGER PIGEON is now extinct. Up to the second half of the last century these pigeons existed in millions, breeding in vast flocks in the beech and oak forests from southern Canada down to the northern parts of Mississippi and Virginia. Audubon claims to have witnessed a flock of over one million birds one day in 1813, near Louisville.

However, their gregarious habits made them very vulnerable to predation by man, and they were exploited as a commercial food resource to such an extent that in a period of less than fifty years the mighty flocks were completely exterminated. The last wild Passenger Pigeon was shot in 1907, and the last known example in captivity died in Cincinnati Zoological Gardens in 1914.

PLATE 62.

Passenger Pigeon Male 1. F. 2.
Columba Migratoria.

Drawn from Nature & Published by John J. Audubon. F.R.S.E. F.L.S. M.W.S.

Engraved by R. Havell Junʳ Printed & Coloured by R. Havell Senʳ London __ 1829

Peregrine Falcon

Falco peregrinus

THERE ARE SEVENTEEN species of peregrine distributed worldwide, and the pair in this illustration are from the northern part of North America. Called here by Audubon the Great Footed Hawk, and often known in North America as the Duck Hawk, its breeding range is from Alaska and Greenland to Lower California, Tennessee and Mexico. Peregrines winter from Vancouver Island and Massachussetts to the West Indies and Panama.

About seventeen inches long, the American *Falco peregrinus* is to be found on crags or cliffs especially near rivers, lakes and the sea. In the winter it may frequent tall buildings where it helps keep down the numbers of pigeons. They will also take small mammals. They do not build nests, but lay three to four eggs in scrapes or in abandoned nests of other species.

PLATE 16.

Great Footed Hawk. No. 16.

FALCO PEREGRINUS.

Drawn from Nature and Published by John J. Audubon, F.R.S.E. M.W.S.

Engraved, Printed & Coloured by R. Havell & Son, London.

Gyrfalcon

Falco rusticolus

GYRFALCONS are the largest representatives of the genus *Falco* and breed in the Arctic. They may winter as far south as Washington and Connecticut.

There are two colour forms, one almost pure white with dark primaries and a few flecks, and the other more usual colouring consisting of brownish-grey upper parts and a whitish breast with dark, drop-like markings. They are about two feet in length with a wingspan of four feet. As with other falcons, their principal prey are birds taken in flight. They lay three to four eggs in scrapes.

PLATE CCCLXVI

Drawn from Nature by J. J. Audubon, F.R.S. F.L.S.

Engraved, Printed, and Coloured by R. Havell, 1837.

Iceland or Jer Falcon.
FALCO ISLANDICUS, *Lath.*
Female Birds.

Little Blue Heron

Florida caerulea

THIS SMALL HERON breeds from new Jersey and Arkansas to Central America, wintering from North Carolina and Texas southwards. It may wander northward in late summer, sometimes beyond the Canadian border.

Only about two feet in length, adults are deep blue with maroon neck and dark legs. They inhabit swamps, marshes and their environs.

PLATE. CCCVII.

Blue Crane, or Heron.
ARDEA CÆRULEA.
1. Adult. 2. Young plumage. 2. Young second Year.
View near Charleston, S.C.

Drawn from Nature by J.J. Audubon. F.R.S. F.L.S.
Engraved, Printed & Coloured by R.Havell 1834.

Atlantic Puffin

Fratercula Arctica

THESE highly specialized birds spend the greater part of the year at sea, breeding from Greenland and Labrador to Maine; also from Norway and the British Isles to Portugal. It winters to New York occasionally (Montauk Point), Morocco and the Azores.

Puffins breed on lonely coasts and islands, laying one egg under rock or in a burrow excavated by other birds or by rabbits. It is about a foot in length and has a large colourful bill which has earned it the name 'Sea Parrot'. It has a bumblebee-like flight and feeds almost exclusively on fish.

PLATE CCXIII

Drawn from Nature by J.J. Audubon. F.R.S. F.L.S.

Engraved, Printed & Coloured by R. Havell 1834.

Puffin. MORMON ARCTICUS. 1. Male. 2. Female.

Common Loon

Gavia immer

KNOWN ALSO as the Great Northern Diver, this bird has a circumpolar breeding range, and formerly extended as far south as Illinois and Pennsylvania. It winters from the Great Lakes and Maine to the Gulf coast, and from Alaska to California.

It is a large bird, about three feet in length, with a dark back and light underparts, and inhabits coastal waters and lakes. An expert swimmer and diver, it is well adapted to prey on fish, aquatic insects and frogs, and in winter will take crustaceans and molluscs as well. It cannot walk on land but at nesting time must use its bill and wings to inch over the ground. It has a strange carrying call likened to laughter, or sometimes even the neighing of horses. The usual egg clutch is two eggs in ill-concealed nests.

PLATE CCCVI.

Great Northern Diver or Loon.
COLYMBUS GLACIALIS, L.
Adult 1. Young in Winter 2.

Whooping Crane
Grus americana

THE AMERICAN WHOOPING CRANE formerly bred from Mackenzie and Hudson Bay to Nebraska and Iowa, and in migration was not uncommon from New England to Georgia. It wintered from the Gulf states to Mexico.

This beautiful species measures up to five feet in length, but is now nearly extinct, partly because the population increases slowly, even in protected environments; the female crane lays only two eggs per year.

Hooping Crane. GRUS AMERICANA. *Adult Male.*

Scarlet Ibis

Guara rubra (Eudocimus ruber)

THE RANGE of this remarkably colourful wader is principally tropical South America, but it is occasionally seen in New Mexico, Texas, Louisiana and Florida.

About 20-22 inches in length, the Scarlet Ibis may be readily reared in captivity, though the vivid plumage may fade if the birds are not fed their natural diet, which includes shrimps as well as fish, insects and molluscs. In the wild, it nests in colonies, laying two eggs. The cry is harsh and high-pitched, but is seldom heard.

PLATE CCCXCVII

Scarlet Ibis.
IBIS RUBRA. *Vieill.*
1. Adult Male. 2. Young Second Autumn.

California Condor

Gymnogyps californicanus

THE RARE California Condor (a variety of vulture, and so called by Audubon here) ranges from California west of the Great Basin and desert regions, and north-western Lower California.

This huge bird is over four feet long and its wingspan measures up to ten feet. It lives in undisturbed mountain areas laying one egg in a sketchy nest of twigs. It does not breed until it is at least six years old, and the young cannot fly until they are about a year old. Condors are voracious eaters and prefer carrion, but they will attack living animals as large as deer. They are vigorously protected as they are on the verge of extinction.

PLATE CCCCXXVI

Californian Vulture
CATHARTES CALIFORNIANUS, Illiger.
Old Male.

Bald Eagle

Haliaetus leucocephalus

THE BREEDING RANGE of the American Bald or White-headed Eagle (bald being used in the sense of white as in 'piebald') extends from Alaska and Labrador to Lower California and Florida. The northern species, found chiefly in Canada, is slightly larger than the southern.

It is about three feet in length, with a wingspan of about seven feet, and builds its nest or eerie of sticks at a vantage point high in a tree or on a cliff, usually near water. It feeds chiefly on fish (it sometimes robs ospreys of their catch) and rodents. Said to mate for life, it usually has two eaglets which do not develop adult markings until the third year, when they leave the parental nest to seek their own territories and mates.

PLATE 31

White-headed Eagle. Male.
FALCO LEUCOCEPHALUS.
Fish Crow.—Yellow and Cat.

Bald Eagle

Haliaetus leucocephalus

THIS ILLUSTRATION of the White-headed or Bald Eagle, fully described on the previous page, shows an immature individual, still without the white head and tail which distinguish the full-grown bird.

White-headed Eagle.
FALCO LEUCOCEPHALUS, Linn.
Young.

Louisiana Heron

Hydranassa tricolor

AUDUBON called this bird 'the lady of the waters'. It breeds from North Carolina and Lower California to the West Indies and Central America. It winters from Lower California and South Carolina southwards.

Inhabiting tidal mudflats, coastal swamps, marshes and mangrove swamps, it feeds mainly on fish captured with a quick stab of its beak while wading in fairly deep water. About two feet in length, it lays three to five eggs in heronries in low nests.

PLATE CCXVII

Louisiana Heron. ARDEA LUDOVICIANA: Wils. *Male adult.*

Drawn from Nature by J. J. Audubon. F.R.S. F.L.S.

Engraved, Printed, & Coloured, by R. Havell, 1834.

Great Black-backed Gull

Larus marinus

THE GREAT BLACK-BACKED GULL breeds from Labrador and Greenland to Maine, and is also native to the British Isles, Scandinavia and Russia. It winters from Greenland to the Great Lakes and Delaware Bay, and even as far afield as the coast of Senegal.

Rocky coasts, lakes, ocean shores and rivers are its favourite habitat. The food is chiefly carrion, but it will take eggs and young birds as well. It lays two to three eggs in a ground nest of grass or rubbish. The call is a deep *kaa-h*. It may be successfully tamed.

Drawn from Nature by J.J.Audubon. F.R.S. F.L.S.

Engraved, Printed, & Coloured, by R. Havell. London 1843.

Black Backed Gull.
LARUS MARINUS.

Marbled Godwit

Limosa fedoa

THE BREEDING RANGE of the Marbled Godwit extends from Alberta and Manitoba to South Dakota. Like the other three species of Godwit, it will travel great distances in its winter ranging, and may be found from California and Georgia to Peru.

Principally a prairie dweller, the habitat has been encroached upon to the detriment of this species, though it is more common in the West. It is about seventeen inches long, and lays three to four eggs. It has a characteristic *go-wit, go-wit, go-wit* call.

PLATE CCXXXVII.

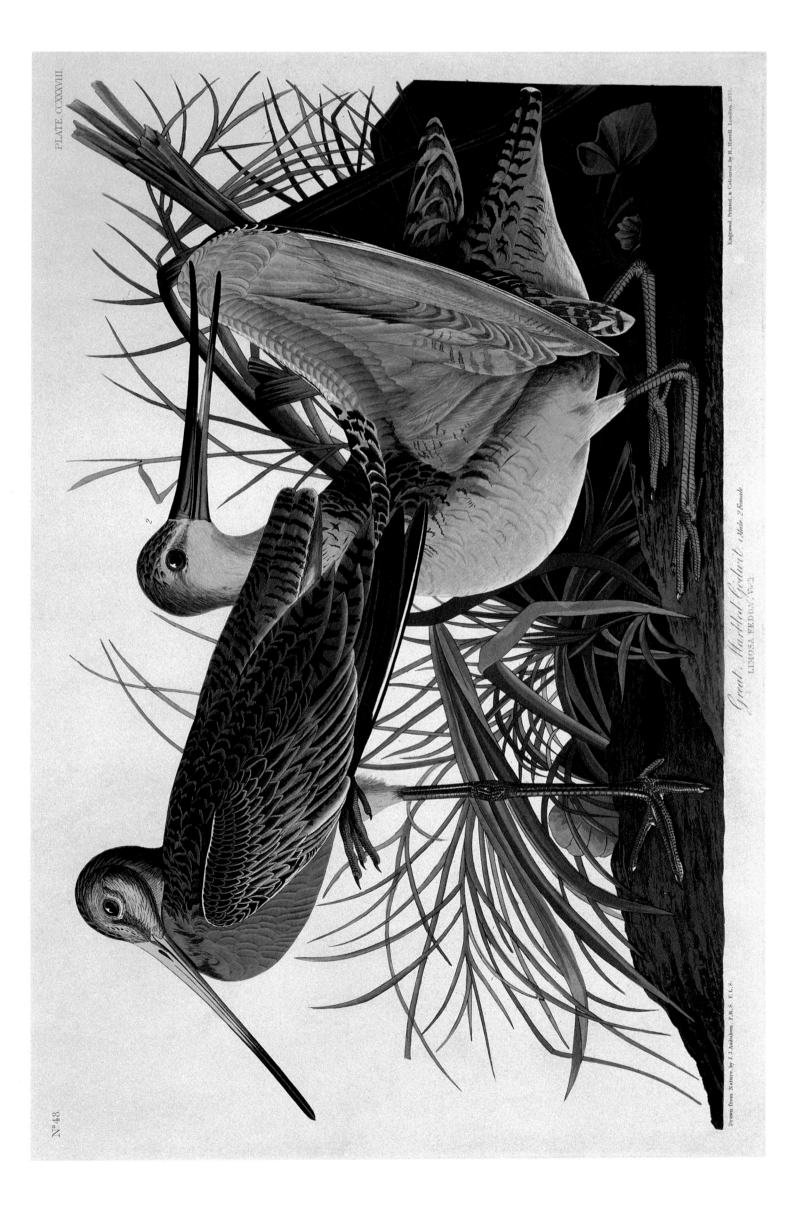

Drawn from Nature. by J.J.Audubon. F.R.S. F.L.S.

Great Marbled Godwit. 1 Male. 2 Female.
LIMOSA FEDOA. N°-21.

Engraved, Printed, & Coloured, by R. Havell, London, 1835.

Mockingbird

Mimus polyglottos

THIS PRE-EMINENT SONGSTER of all North American birds ranges from California, Wyoming and New Jersey to Mexico and Florida, and has been introduced into Bermuda.

It is about ten inches long, and is most commonly found near farms and gardens. Its song, usually delivered from a high, exposed perch, is unrestricted as to time or season and includes phrases from other birds' songs (of which it will repeat as many as 30 in succession), with imitations of familiar sounds as well as a melodious song of its own. It lays three to six eggs in a bulky nest.

The Mocking Bird. 1 Male. 2 F.
TURDUS POLYGLOTTUS.
Plant Vulgo. Yellow Jessamin.

Rattlesnake.
CROTALUS HORRIDUS.

Drawn from Nature and Published by John J. Audubon, F.R.S.E. M.W.S.

Engraved, Printed and Coloured by R. Havell & Son, London.

Osprey

Pandion haliaetus

THE OSPREY or Fish Hawk is distributed throughout the world with the exception of New Zealand, the Hawaiian Islands and the frozen Polar regions. In North America it breeds from Alaska and Labrador to Lower California and Florida. It winters from Lower California and Florida to the West Indies and Central America.

Ospreys live in colonies near lakes, rivers or bays, building large nests of sticks and vegetation. In treeless territory, the birds may make use of telegraph poles, causing much trouble by short-circuiting the wires. Poles surmounted with old wagon wheels are now erected for their use. They live entirely on fish, diving into the water from 50 to 200 feet above, and the dive frequently carries the bird far beneath the surface. Two to four eggs are laid. The voice is a high whistle as though from escaping steam.

PLATE 81.

Fish Hawk

Vulgo Weat. Fish.

FALCO HALIÆTUS.

Drawn from Nature and Published by John J. Audubon, F.R.S. F.L.S. &c.

Engraved, Printed & Coloured by R. Havell June 1830

White Pelican

Pelecanus erythrorhynchos

ALSO KNOWN as the Rough-billed Pelican, this bird breeds from British Columbia, the Great Slave Lake and Manitoba to California and Texas. It winters from California and Florida to Panama.

The White Pelican inhabits lakes, rivers and coastal areas, feeding off fish which it scoops up whilst swimming (the smaller brown pelican dives from the air for its prey). It is about five feet long with a wingspan of eight to ten feet. In the breeding season it develops an irregular-shaped upright, horny plate on the culmen, as shown in this illustration.

PLATE CCCXI.

Drawn from Nature by J. J. Audubon, F.R.S. F.L.S.

Engraved, Printed & Coloured by R. Havell, 1836.

American White Pelican.
PELICANUS AMERICANUS, Aud.
Male Adult.

Flamingo

Phoenicopterus ruber

THE RANGE of the American or greater flamingo is the Atlantic coast of subtropical and tropical America. It breeds from the Bahamas to Guiana and Peru. It was formerly a visitor near the southern tip of the Florida Peninsula, but is now of casual occurrence on the Florida coast.

Flamingos are invariably found on brackish or salt-water lakes or lagoons, and they obtain their food – chiefly blue-green algae and diatoms – by straining water and mud through the lamellae, which are small, hair-like filters lining their mandibles. The birds are about four feet in length, with a wingspan of five to six feet. They lay one egg in a mud nest.

Drawn from Nature by J. J. Audubon, F.R.S. F.L.S.

Engraved, Printed and Coloured by Robt Havell. 1838.

1.—Profile view of Bill at its greatest extension.
2.—Superior front view of upper Mandible.
3.—Interior front view of upper Mandible.
4.—Inferior front view of lower Mandible.
5.—Interior front view of lower Mandible with the Tongue in.

American Flamingo.
PHŒNICOPTERUS RUBER, *Linn.*
Old Male.

6.—Profile view of Tongue.
7.—Superior front view of Tongue.
8.—Inferior front view of Tongue.
9.—Perpendicular front view of the feet fully expanded.

Double-crested Cormorant

Phalocrocorax auritus

THIS common North American cormorant has a breeding range which extends from Kodiak Island and Newfoundland to Lower California and the Isle of Pines. It winters on the Atlantic coast from Virginia southwards.

Called here by Audubon the Florida Cormorant, it will inhabit lakes, interior swamps, bays and coastal islands, subsisting principally on fish which it pursues underwater. It measures two to three feet in length and lays two to seven eggs in colonies on the ground or in trees.

PLATE. CCLII

Florida Cormorant.
CARBO FLORIDANUS,
Male Adult. Spring Drefs. *Var. Florida Keys.*

Drawn from Nature by J.J.Audubon. F.R.S. F.L.S.

Engraved, Printed & Coloured by R. Havell London 1835.

Arctic Three-toed Woodpecker

Picoides arcticus

RANGING from Alaska and Quebec to California and Maine, this bird may be found further south in winter.

The bird is about ten inches long, and it is the male which has the yellow patch on the head. It lives in northern coniferous forests, and its presence may be surmised by barkless trees which it peels in its search for food, principally borers and other insects, as well as berries. It generally lays four eggs, and these are concealed in the nest which is built inside a hole in a tree.

PLATE. CXXXII.

Drawn from Nature by J.J.Audubon, F.R.S. F.L.S.

Three-toed Woodpecker, PICUS TRIDACTYLUS, Linn. *Males, 1. Female, 2.*

Engraved,Printed,& Coloured, by R.Havell, London 1832.

Pied-billed Grebe

Podilymbus podiceps

THIS is perhaps the best-known representative of the grebe family in North America. It breeds locally from British Columbia and Nova Scotia to Mexico. Its winter range is from British Columbia and New York southward.

The Pied-billed Grebe's preferred habitat is one of lakes, rivers and marshes or bogs with weedy shores. It measures about 13 inches in length and has a loud, almost cuckoo-like call. It eats crustaceans, fish, aquatic insects and plants, and has an unexplained habit of swallowing feathers. Grebes have elaborate courtship rituals including dancing in pairs on the water. They lay six to eight eggs on a nest that is frequently floating.

Locally this bird is known as the Dobchick, Dabchick, Water Witch or Didapper, and sometimes as the Hell-diver because of its ability to vanish under the water.

PLATE. CCXLVIII.

Engraved, Printed, & Coloured by R. Havell London 1835.

American Pied-bill Dobchick.
PODICEPS CAROLINENSIS.

Drawn from Nature by J.J.Audubon. F.R.S. F.L.S.

Purple Gallinule

Porphyrula martinica

THE PURPLE GALLINULE will breed from Texas and South Carolina to Argentina, and winter from Texas and Florida southwards.

This bird lives in swamps, hunting its food mainly at night. This consists of insects, molluscs and seeds. Although it is a migratory species, it has small wings and is a weak flyer. In general, it relies on concealment to escape the predatory attentions of other species. It lays five to eight eggs in low, grassy rushes in marshes.

PLATE. CCCV.

Drawn from Nature by J.J. Audubon, F.R.S. F.L.S.

Engraved, Printed, & Coloured by R. Havell. 1836

Purple Gallinule.
GALLINULA MARTINICA, Gmel.
Adult Male spring plumage.

American Redstart

Setophaga ruticilla

ALTHOUGH the American Redstart breeds from British Columbia, Mackenzie and Newfoundland to Oregon, Arkansas and Georgia, it winters in Central and northern South America from Mexico to Guiana and also in the West Indies.

This small bird, which measures only just over five inches, inhabits deciduous woods and orchards near water. It builds exquisite nests in which it lays three to five eggs, and its cry is a thin, clear *swee-swee-swee*.

PLATE 40.

American Redstart Male 1. F.2.

MUSCICAPA RUTICILLA.

Plant Vulgo. Scrub Elm.

Ostrya Virginica.

Drawn from Nature and Published by John J. Audubon. F.R.S.E. F.L.S. M.W.S.
Engraved by Rob.ᵗ Havell, Jun.ʳ Printed & Coloured by R. Havell. Sen.ʳ London. 1828.

Kingbird

Tyrannus tryannus

THE KINGBIRD is a flycatcher (of which there are 365 species distributed throughout the Americas) breeding from British Columbia and Nova Scotia to New Mexico and Florida. It winters from Mexico to Peru and Bolivia.

It lives in woods, orchards and thickets, often close to civilization. Although this bird is also called the Bee Martin, it actually prefers other small insects which it takes on the wing, and Audubon knew it as the Tyrant Flycatcher. It lays three to five eggs in high bushes and trees. Its Latin name *Tyrannus tyrannus* derives from its habit of fearlessly driving off crows, hawks and other large birds which threaten its nest.

PLATE 79.

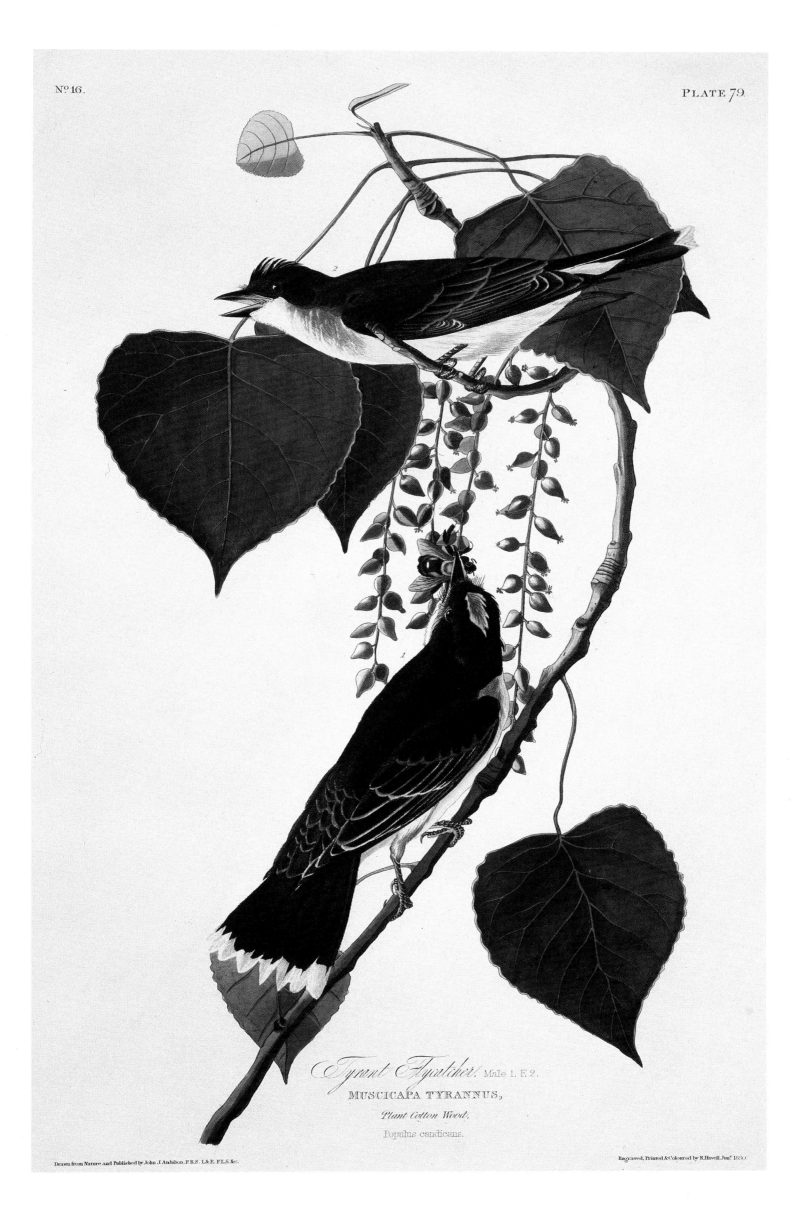

Tyrant Flycatcher. Male 1. F. 2.

MUSCICAPA TYRANNUS,

Plant Cotton Wood.

Populus candicans.

Drawn from Nature and Published by John J. Audubon, F.R.S. L.& E. F.L.S. &c.

Engraved, Printed & Coloured by R.Havell, Junʳ. 1830.